THE WEALTH BLUEPRINT

A Guide to Financial Mastery

CVO, UPTRENDR

Contents

Disclaimer

The content provided in this book is for educational and informational purposes only and should not be considered as financial advice. The information presented is based on the author's knowledge and research at the time of writing, and it may not be suitable for every individual's specific financial situation.

Readers are advised to consult with a qualified financial professional or advisor before making any financial decisions or implementing any strategies discussed in this book. The author and publisher disclaim any liability or responsibility for any actions taken by readers based on the information provided in this book.

The content of this book is not intended to substitute professional financial advice or guidance. Each individual's financial circumstances are unique, and readers should carefully consider their own financial goals, risk tolerance, and consult with appropriate professionals to make informed decisions.

Introduction

The introductory chapter sets the stage for the book by highlighting the importance of financial literacy in today's world. It emphasizes that financial literacy is not just for experts or professionals but is a vital skill for individuals of all backgrounds and walks of life. It introduces the concept of financial literacy as the knowledge and understanding of personal finance concepts, tools, and strategies that enable individuals to make informed financial decisions and achieve their financial goals.

Defining Financial Literacy:
Financial literacy refers to the knowledge and skills necessary to make informed financial decisions. It encompasses understanding concepts such as budgeting, saving, investing, and managing credit and debt. With financial literacy, individuals can gain control over their finances, plan for the future, and achieve their financial goals.

Why Do We Need Financial Literacy?
This section explores the reasons why financial literacy is crucial in our lives. It highlights the challenges individuals face due to complex financial systems, rising personal debt, and economic uncertainties. It

emphasizes that financial literacy empowers individuals to make sound financial decisions, effectively manage their money, and navigate financial challenges. It also stresses that financial literacy promotes financial well-being, reduces financial stress, and improves overall quality of life.

The Impact of Financial Illiteracy:
This part delves into the consequences of financial illiteracy. It discusses the potential pitfalls individuals may face, such as falling into debt traps, making poor investment choices, or being vulnerable to financial scams. It highlights the negative impact of financial illiteracy on individuals' financial security, retirement planning, and ability to achieve financial goals. By illustrating the potential risks and consequences, this section emphasizes the urgency of improving financial literacy.

Benefits of Financial Literacy:
This section explores the numerous benefits that come with financial literacy. It discusses how financial literacy enables individuals to create and maintain budgets, effectively manage debt, build savings, and plan for retirement. It highlights the positive impact on long-term wealth accumulation, financial independence, and the ability to seize financial opportunities. Financial literacy also empowers individuals to make informed decisions about major life events, such as buying a

home, starting a family, or pursuing higher education.

The Role of Financial Education:
This part discusses the role of financial education in promoting financial literacy. It highlights the need for comprehensive financial education in schools, workplaces, and communities. It emphasizes that financial education should start at a young age and continue throughout one's lifetime. The chapter emphasizes that financial education provides individuals with the knowledge and skills to make informed financial decisions, develop healthy financial habits, and adapt to changing financial landscapes.

This book focuses on the above four main pillars of improving financial literacy. By exploring the importance of financial literacy, the reasons why we need it, the impact of financial illiteracy, the benefits it brings, and the role of financial education, readers gain a comprehensive understanding of why financial literacy is a critical skill to develop. This chapter lays the foundation for the rest of the book, setting the context for the subsequent chapters that delve into specific aspects of financial literacy and provide practical guidance for improvement.

Why Do We Need Financial Literacy?

The introductory section of Chapter 2 provides an overview of why financial literacy is essential in our lives. It emphasizes that financial literacy is not just a skill for managing money but a fundamental life skill that impacts various aspects of our personal and professional lives.

Making Informed Financial Decisions:
This section explores the importance of making informed financial decisions. It highlights that financial decisions have long-term consequences and can significantly impact our financial well-being. It emphasizes that being financially literate allows individuals to analyze options, consider risks and rewards, and make choices aligned with their goals and values. Making informed financial decisions helps individuals avoid impulsive or detrimental choices and optimize their financial resources.

Building Financial Stability and Security:
Financial stability and security are key reasons why financial literacy is crucial. This section explains that financial literacy equips individuals with the knowledge and skills to manage their finances effectively, plan for emergencies, and build a financial cushion.

It emphasizes that being financially literate allows individuals to create budgets, save for future goals, and develop strategies to handle unexpected expenses. Financial stability and security provide peace of mind and a solid foundation for individuals and their families.

Navigating Complex Financial Systems:
This part discusses the complexity of modern financial systems and the importance of financial literacy in navigating them. It highlights that financial systems, including banking, investments, taxes, and insurance, involve intricate processes, regulations, and terminology. Being financially literate allows individuals to understand and navigate these systems with confidence. It helps individuals avoid costly mistakes, understand their rights and obligations, and make informed choices when dealing with financial institutions and professionals.

Preparing for Financial Goals and Milestones:
Financial goals and milestones play a significant role in our lives, such as buying a home, starting a family, or retiring comfortably. This section emphasizes that financial literacy is essential for planning and preparing for these milestones. It discusses how financial literacy helps individuals set realistic goals, create effective saving and investment strategies, and overcome financial obstacles. It highlights that being financially literate enables individuals to align their financial

decisions with their goals, track their progress, and make adjustments when necessary.

Empowering Individuals and Promoting Independence: Financial literacy empowers individuals to take control of their financial lives and promotes independence. This section explains that being financially literate allows individuals to rely less on external support or guidance when it comes to managing their finances. It enables individuals to assess their financial situations, make independent decisions, and advocate for their financial interests. Financial literacy fosters a sense of empowerment and self-reliance, enabling individuals to navigate financial challenges and pursue their aspirations.

By exploring the importance of making informed financial decisions, building financial stability and security, navigating complex financial systems, preparing for financial goals and milestones, and empowering individuals and promoting independence, readers gain a deeper understanding of the significance of financial literacy. This chapter underscores the practical benefits and positive impact that financial literacy brings to individuals' lives.

The Foundations of Financial Literacy

Money Management Skills:
Effective money management skills are the cornerstone of financial literacy. It involves understanding how to handle your income, expenses, and savings. By mastering money management, individuals can gain control over their finances and make informed decisions about their financial priorities. This includes creating a comprehensive budget that outlines income sources and categorizes expenses, tracking spending habits, and identifying areas for potential savings. Money management skills also encompass developing strategies for saving and investing, setting financial goals, and managing financial resources efficiently.

Budgeting and Tracking Expenses:
Budgeting is a fundamental aspect of financial literacy. It involves creating a spending plan that aligns with your income and financial goals. A well-designed budget helps you allocate your income towards essential expenses, such as housing, utilities, and food, as well as discretionary spending and savings. By tracking expenses, you gain insights into your spending patterns and can identify areas where you can cut back or make adjustments. Tracking expenses can be done manually using a notbook or spreadsheet, or through various

budgeting apps and online tools that automate the process. Regularly reviewing and adjusting your budget ensures that it remains aligned with your financial priorities.

Saving and Emergency Funds:
Saving money is a critical component of financial literacy. It involves setting aside a portion of your income for future use or unexpected expenses. Saving can help you achieve short-term goals, such as purchasing a car or taking a vacation, as well as long-term goals, such as retirement or buying a home. Financial literacy emphasizes the importance of establishing an emergency fund—a readily accessible savings account to cover unexpected financial setbacks, such as medical expenses or job loss. By consistently saving and building emergency funds, individuals can mitigate financial stress and have a safety net for unforeseen circumstances.

By mastering money management skills, including budgeting, expense tracking, and saving, individuals can gain control over their financial lives and make informed decisions about their financial priorities. These foundational skills serve as the building blocks for further financial literacy development.

Building Financial Knowledge

Understanding Financial Terminology:
To improve financial literacy, it is crucial to familiarize yourself with key financial terminology. This includes terms like compound interest, inflation, diversification, and asset allocation. Understanding these terms allows individuals to make more informed decisions about their finances and navigate conversations with financial professionals or institutions. For example, knowing what compound interest means helps individuals understand how their savings or investments can grow over time, while understanding inflation helps individuals assess the impact of rising prices on their purchasing power. By deepening their knowledge of financial terminology, individuals can enhance their ability to comprehend and engage in financial discussions effectively.

Basic Banking and Financial Services:
Financial literacy involves understanding the basic banking services available to individuals. This includes opening and managing bank accounts, such as checking and savings accounts, and utilizing online banking services. Knowing how to navigate online banking platforms enables individuals to monitor their account balances, track transactions, and transfer funds

conveniently. Additionally, understanding different financial services offered by banks, such as loans, mortgages, and credit cards, empowers individuals to make informed decisions when considering borrowing or utilizing credit facilities.

Credit and Debt Management:
Credit and debt are integral parts of personal finance, and developing knowledge in this area is essential for financial literacy. Understanding the concept of credit, credit scores, and credit reports is crucial when applying for loans, credit cards, or other forms of credit. By comprehending how credit scores are calculated and how they impact borrowing costs, individuals can work towards maintaining a good credit history. Debt management is also a significant aspect of financial literacy, as it involves strategies for responsible borrowing, managing debt repayment plans, and avoiding excessive debt burdens. Knowledge of interest rates, loan terms, and repayment options allows individuals to make informed decisions about taking on debt and develop strategies to pay it off efficiently.

By building financial knowledge in areas such as financial terminology, basic banking services, and credit and debt management, individuals can gain the necessary skills to navigate financial systems and make informed decisions. This deeper understanding enables individuals to optimize their financial resources, minimize financial risks, and seize opportunities that align with their financial goals.

Investing with Financial Literacy

The Mindset of a Successful Investor:
A successful investor possesses a specific mindset that guides their investment decisions. This mindset includes factors such as patience, discipline, risk tolerance, and a long-term perspective. Successful investors understand that investing is a journey that requires diligence, research, and the ability to stay focused despite market fluctuations. They embrace the concept of diversification, spreading their investments across different asset classes to minimize risk. Additionally, successful investors have the courage to stay invested during periods of market volatility and avoid making impulsive decisions based on short-term market movements. By adopting a mindset aligned with long-term wealth accumulation and a disciplined approach to investing, individuals can increase their chances of achieving their financial goals.

Types of Investments:
Financial literacy encompasses knowledge of various investment options available to individuals. These options include stocks, bonds, mutual funds, real estate, and retirement accounts. Understanding the characteristics, risks, and potential returns of each investment type is essential for making informed

investment decisions. For instance, stocks represent ownership in a company, while bonds are debt instruments. Mutual funds provide diversification through a pool of investments managed by professionals, and real estate can generate income through rental properties or appreciation in property value. Retirement accounts, such as 401(k)s and IRAs, offer tax advantages and long-term wealth accumulation opportunities. By understanding the different investment options, individuals can align their investment choices with their financial goals, risk tolerance, and time horizon.

Evaluating Investment Opportunities:
Investing wisely requires the ability to evaluate and analyze investment opportunities effectively. This involves conducting thorough research, analyzing financial statements, assessing market trends, and understanding industry dynamics. Fundamental analysis examines a company's financial health, competitive position, and growth potential, while technical analysis utilizes historical price and volume data to predict future market movements. Evaluating investment opportunities also involves understanding the associated risks and rewards, considering factors such as liquidity, diversification, and the potential for capital gains or income. Real-life case studies and examples of successful investment strategies can provide valuable insights into the evaluation process

and highlight the importance of due diligence.

By understanding the mindset of a successful investor, familiarizing oneself with various investment options, and developing the skills to evaluate investment opportunities, individuals can make more informed investment decisions aligned with their financial goals and risk tolerance. This knowledge empowers individuals to grow their wealth, build a diversified investment portfolio, and navigate the dynamic landscape of the financial markets.

Navigating the World of Credit

Credit Scores and Reports:
Credit scores play a crucial role in accessing credit and obtaining favorable terms. A credit score is a numerical representation of an individual's creditworthiness and is based on factors such as payment history, credit utilization, length of credit history, types of credit, and new credit inquiries. Understanding how credit scores are calculated and the factors that influence them is essential. Monitoring credit reports regularly helps individuals identify errors or discrepancies that could negatively impact their credit scores. By maintaining a good credit score, individuals can access better loan terms, lower interest rates, and higher credit limits.

Managing Credit Cards and Loans:
Credit cards and loans are common financial tools that require responsible management. This involves understanding the terms and conditions of credit cards and loans, such as interest rates, repayment schedules, and fees. Using credit cards responsibly includes paying bills on time, avoiding carrying high balances, and utilizing credit wisely. Similarly, managing loans entails making regular payments, staying within budget, and considering the impact on overall debt load. By practicing responsible credit card and loan

management, individuals can maintain good credit standing and avoid unnecessary debt burdens.

Avoiding Debt Traps:
Debt traps can quickly lead to financial instability and stress. Common debt traps include high-interest payday loans, predatory lending practices, and excessive use of credit cards. Understanding the risks associated with these types of debt is vital for financial literacy. Strategies for avoiding debt traps include budgeting, building emergency funds, seeking alternatives to high-interest loans, and being cautious of excessive borrowing. By making informed decisions and prioritizing debt reduction, individuals can avoid falling into debt traps and maintain financial stability.

By developing a deep understanding of credit scores and reports, managing credit cards and loans responsibly, and avoiding debt traps, individuals can navigate the world of credit with confidence and minimize financial risks. Financial literacy in this area empowers individuals to access credit when needed, maintain a healthy credit profile, and avoid unnecessary debt burdens.

Long-Term Financial Planning

Retirement Planning:
Retirement planning is a crucial aspect of financial literacy, ensuring individuals can maintain their desired lifestyle during their retirement years. It involves setting goals, estimating retirement expenses, and determining the amount of savings required to achieve those goals. Retirement planning also considers factors such as retirement account contributions, Social Security benefits, and potential investment growth. Understanding retirement savings vehicles, such as 401(k)s and IRAs, helps individuals make informed decisions about maximizing contributions and taking advantage of employer matching programs. By engaging in retirement planning early and regularly reassessing goals and strategies, individuals can work towards a secure and fulfilling retirement.

Insurance and Risk Management:
Insurance serves as a risk management tool, protecting individuals and their assets from unforeseen events. Financial literacy includes understanding the different types of insurance, such as health, life, auto, and homeowners insurance. It involves evaluating insurance needs, comparing policies, and selecting coverage that aligns with individual circumstances. Understanding

policy terms, deductibles, and premiums helps individuals make informed choices while considering their budget and risk tolerance. By obtaining adequate insurance coverage, individuals can safeguard their financial well-being and protect against potential financial hardships arising from accidents, illnesses, or property damage.

Estate Planning:
Estate planning involves the orderly distribution of assets and the management of financial affairs after an individual's passing. Financial literacy includes understanding the components of an estate plan, such as wills, trusts, power of attorney, and healthcare directives. It entails clarifying beneficiaries, minimizing tax implications, and ensuring the smooth transfer of assets to intended recipients. By engaging in estate planning, individuals can protect their legacy, minimize potential conflicts among beneficiaries, and ensure their wishes are carried out effectively. Seeking guidance from legal professionals experienced in estate planning can help navigate complex laws and regulations.

By focusing on long-term financial planning, individuals can establish a solid foundation for financial security. Financial literacy in these areas allows individuals to make informed decisions, protect their assets and loved ones, and plan for a financially stable future.

Financial Literacy for Entrepreneurs

Starting a Business: Financial Considerations:
Entrepreneurs embarking on a business venture need to understand the financial considerations involved. This includes conducting market research to assess the viability of the business idea, creating a comprehensive business plan, and estimating start-up costs. Financial considerations also involve identifying potential sources of financing, such as personal savings, loans, grants, or investment capital. Understanding the financial aspects of starting a business helps entrepreneurs make informed decisions, set realistic expectations, and secure the necessary resources for a successful launch.

Business Financing Options:
Entrepreneurs have various financing options available to fund their business operations. These options include traditional bank loans, Small Business Administration (SBA) loans, venture capital, angel investors, crowdfunding, or bootstrapping. Each financing option has its own advantages, requirements, and implications for ownership and control. Financial literacy enables entrepreneurs to evaluate these options, understand the terms and conditions, and determine which financing method aligns best with their business goals and risk tolerance. By exploring different financing

avenues, entrepreneurs can secure the necessary capital to start or expand their businesses.

Financial Management for Small Business Owners:
Financial management is critical for the success of a small business. It involves budgeting, cash flow management, financial forecasting, and monitoring key financial metrics. Small business owners need to understand how to create and manage budgets, track revenues and expenses, and make informed financial decisions. Financial literacy also encompasses understanding financial statements, such as income statements, balance sheets, and cash flow statements, which provide valuable insights into the business's financial health. By effectively managing their finances, small business owners can optimize profitability, make strategic decisions, and ensure the long-term sustainability of their ventures.

By addressing the financial considerations of starting a business, exploring different financing options, and emphasizing the importance of financial management, entrepreneurs can enhance their financial literacy and increase the likelihood of building successful and sustainable businesses.

Financial Literacy for Different Life Stages

Financial Literacy for Students:
Students can benefit greatly from developing financial literacy skills early on. This involves understanding the basics of personal finance, such as budgeting, saving, and managing expenses. Financial literacy for students also includes knowledge about student loans, scholarships, and grants, as well as the importance of building good credit. By gaining financial literacy at a young age, students can make informed decisions about their education, manage their money effectively, and establish a solid financial foundation for the future.

Financial Literacy for Young Professionals:
As young professionals embark on their careers, financial literacy becomes increasingly important. This includes understanding workplace benefits, such as retirement plans, health insurance options, and employee stock purchase plans. Young professionals also need to develop strategies for managing their income, setting financial goals, and building emergency funds. Financial literacy for young professionals involves navigating the complexities of taxes, optimizing employer-sponsored retirement plans, and making informed decisions about investing for the future. By developing strong financial habits early in their careers,

young professionals can set themselves up for long-term financial success.

Financial Literacy for Parents and Families:
Parents have unique financial considerations, including managing household expenses, saving for their children's education, and planning for their family's future. Financial literacy for parents involves understanding the costs and benefits of different types of education savings accounts, such as 529 plans or education savings bonds. It also includes strategies for budgeting, teaching children about money, and ensuring adequate insurance coverage to protect the family's financial well-being. By being financially literate, parents can provide their children with a strong financial education and create a stable and secure environment for their family.

Financial Literacy for Seniors:
Seniors face specific financial challenges, such as retirement income planning, healthcare costs, and estate planning. Financial literacy for seniors involves understanding the various sources of retirement income, including Social Security benefits, pensions, and retirement account withdrawals. It also includes making informed decisions about Medicare options, long-term care insurance, and managing healthcare expenses. Estate planning is another crucial aspect, ensuring that assets are distributed according to one's wishes and

minimizing tax implications. By being financially literate, seniors can navigate retirement with confidence, protect their financial well-being, and leave a legacy for future generations.

By addressing financial literacy needs at different life stages, including students, young professionals, parents, and seniors, individuals can develop the knowledge and skills necessary to make informed financial decisions throughout their lives. Financial literacy empowers individuals to adapt to their changing circumstances, maximize financial opportunities, and achieve long-term financial security.

Cultivating a Financially Literate Mindset

Overcoming Common Money Mindset Challenges:
Developing a healthy mindset towards money is essential for financial success. This involves recognizing and overcoming common money mindset challenges such as scarcity mentality, fear of investing, and impulsive spending. Scarcity mentality refers to the belief that there is a limited amount of money available and that financial opportunities are scarce. Overcoming this mindset involves shifting towards an abundance mindset, focusing on opportunities and possibilities. Fear of investing often stems from a lack of knowledge or past negative experiences. By educating oneself about investing and understanding the benefits of long-term investing, individuals can overcome this fear. Impulsive spending can be a result of emotional or impulsive decision-making. Developing self-awareness, setting financial goals, and practicing mindful spending can help overcome this challenge and cultivate better financial habits.

Developing Financial Habits and Discipline:
Building strong financial habits is crucial for long-term financial success. This includes developing discipline in managing money, setting and following a budget, and practicing regular saving. By creating a habit of

automating savings, individuals ensure consistent progress towards their financial goals. Developing discipline also involves being mindful of spending, avoiding unnecessary expenses, and staying committed to the budget. It requires making conscious choices aligned with long-term financial well-being rather than giving in to immediate gratification. By consistently practicing these financial habits, individuals can create a solid foundation for their financial future.

The Importance of Continuous Learning:
Financial literacy is a lifelong journey that requires continuous learning. This involves staying updated on financial trends, understanding new investment strategies, and being aware of changes in laws and regulations. Continuous learning can be achieved through reading financial books, following reputable financial blogs, attending workshops or webinars, and engaging in online courses. It also involves seeking knowledge and guidance from financial professionals who can provide insights and expertise. By embracing a mindset of continuous learning, individuals can adapt to changing financial landscapes, make informed decisions, and stay ahead in their financial journeys.

By addressing common money mindset challenges, developing financial habits and discipline, and embracing continuous learning, individuals can cultivate a financially literate mindset. This mindset allows them to make sound financial decisions, overcome obstacles, and achieve long-term financial success.

Strategies for Improving Financial Literacy

Utilizing Online Resources and Courses:
The internet provides a wealth of resources and educational opportunities to enhance financial literacy. Online platforms offer a wide range of articles, videos, podcasts, and courses on various financial topics. Reputable websites, such as government agencies, financial institutions, and personal finance blogs, can provide reliable information and practical tips. Online courses and webinars hosted by financial experts and institutions offer structured learning experiences tailored to specific areas of financial literacy. By utilizing online resources and courses, individuals can access valuable information, expand their knowledge, and enhance their financial literacy at their own pace.

Seeking Guidance from Financial Professionals:
Financial professionals, such as financial advisors, accountants, and planners, can provide personalized guidance based on individual financial situations. Seeking their expertise can help individuals develop tailored financial plans, navigate complex financial decisions, and receive professional advice. Financial professionals can assist in areas such as retirement planning, tax planning, investment strategies, and risk management. It is important to choose qualified and

trustworthy professionals by considering their credentials, experience, and client testimonials. By engaging with financial professionals, individuals can gain valuable insights and make more informed financial decisions aligned with their goals and values.

Joining Community and Peer Support Groups:
Community and peer support groups can provide valuable opportunities for learning and growth. Online forums, social media groups, or local community organizations focused on financial literacy allow individuals to connect with like-minded individuals and share experiences, challenges, and success stories. Peer support groups provide a platform for discussing financial topics, seeking advice, and exchanging ideas. Participating in workshops, seminars, or local events organized by financial literacy groups also facilitates networking and learning from others' experiences. By joining community and peer support groups, individuals can find encouragement, accountability, and inspiration on their financial literacy journey.

By utilizing online resources and courses, seeking guidance from financial professionals, and joining community and peer support groups, individuals can actively improve their financial literacy. These strategies provide access to valuable knowledge, personalized advice, and a supportive community that can enhance financial decision-making and overall financial well-being.

Conclusion

Embracing Financial Literacy for a Secure Future:
In the concluding chapter, the emphasis is placed on the transformative power of financial literacy and its role in securing a stable future. Financial literacy equips individuals with the knowledge and skills necessary to make informed decisions about their personal finances. By understanding concepts such as budgeting, saving, investing, and risk management, individuals can take control of their financial lives and work towards achieving their financial goals. Financial literacy empowers individuals to create a solid foundation for their financial well-being, reduce financial stress, and build a more secure future for themselves and their families.

Encouraging Financial Literacy in Society:
The importance of promoting financial literacy at a broader level is highlighted in this chapter. Financial education should be integrated into school curriculums, workplace training programs, and community initiatives. By providing accessible financial literacy resources, educational institutions, policymakers, employers, and community organizations can empower individuals from all walks of life to enhance their financial knowledge and skills. Promoting financial literacy creates a ripple effect

that benefits individuals, families, and communities by fostering economic stability, reducing wealth inequalities, and promoting responsible financial behavior.

The book concludes by reiterating the key takeaways and insights gained throughout its chapters. It emphasizes the significance of taking proactive steps towards improving financial literacy and the long-term benefits it brings. By embracing financial literacy, individuals can navigate the complexities of personal finance, make informed decisions, and adapt to the ever-changing financial landscape.

The comprehensive exploration of financial literacy in the book aims to equip readers with practical knowledge, real-life examples, and reputable sources. By providing insights into the importance of financial literacy, the correct mindset for financial success, and strategies for improvement, the book empowers readers to take charge of their financial lives. By incorporating reputable sources and real-life examples, readers can gain valuable insights and actionable strategies that enable them to enhance their financial literacy and secure their financial future.

Resources and Further Reading

Books:
1. "Rich Dad Poor Dad" by Robert Kiyosaki
2. "The Total Money Makeover" by Dave Ramsey
3. "I Will Teach You to Be Rich" by Ramit Sethi
4. "The Millionaire Next Door" by Thomas J. Stanley and William D. Danko
5. "A Random Walk Down Wall Street" by Burton G. Malkiel

Websites and Blogs:
1. Investopedia (www.investopedia.com)
2. The Balance (www.thebalance.com)
3. NerdWallet (www.nerdwallet.com)
4. Financial Planning Association (www.onefpa.org)
5. The Motley Fool (www.fool.com)

www.ingramcontent.com/pod-product-compliance
Lightning Source LLC
Chambersburg PA
CBHW060907260726
48661CB00008B/3501